·WORKBOOK FOR WOMEN·

Saving Your
SECOND
MARRIAGE
Before It Starts

EXPANDED &
UPDATED EDITION

Nine Questions
to Ask Before
— and After — You Remarry

Drs. Les and Leslie Parrott

ZONDERVAN

GRAND RAPIDS, MICHIGAN 49530 U

ZONDERVAN.COM/
AUTHORTRACKER

ZONDERVAN®

Saving Your Second Marriage Before It Starts Workbook for Women
Copyright © 2001, 2006 by Les and Leslie Parrott
Expanded and Updated Edition

Requests for information should be addressed to:
Zondervan, *Grand Rapids, Michigan 49530*

ISBN-10: 0-310-27585-7
ISBN-13: 978-0-310-27585-5

The website addresses recommended throughout this book are offered as a resource to you. These websites are not intended in any way to be or imply an endorsement on the part of Zondervan, nor do we vouch for their content for the life of this book.

Published in association with Yates & Yates, LLP, Attorneys and Counselors, Suite 1000, Literary Agent, Orange, CA.

Printed in the United States of America

06 07 08 09 10 11 12 • 22 21 20 19 18 17 16 15 14 13 12 11 10 9 8 7 6 5 4 3 2 1

Contents

SESSIONS
For Group or Couple Discussion
with the DVD Curriculum

ADDITIONAL SESSIONS
For Couples Considering Remarriage

How to Use This Workbook

We have seen many couples who marry and then wait to see what will happen. This workbook is a tool to help you make the *right* things happen. Its brief exercises and activities, to be completed as you read through *Saving Your Second Marriage Before It Starts*, come from our work in counseling couples and are proven strategies for enriching and developing your relationship. Too often, reading a book can lead to great ideas, but little action. This workbook will help you put feet on the ideas and put them into action. And we believe you will enjoy it! As Shakespeare said, "Joy's soul lies in the doing."

This workbook is to be used in conjunction with your husband's — there is one designed for men and one for women — and it is important that each of you have your own copy. For the best results, each of you should work on the exercises separately, then meet together to discuss your answers.

While there is no one right way to use this workbook, we suggest that you complete the exercises as you encounter them in the book, or soon after you have finished reading the chapter that covers the exercise. In other words, try to complete the exercises for that chapter before moving on to the next one. The point is to integrate the exercises into the process of reading the book. Some of the exercises are designed to be used again and again, helping you continue to improve your communication, for example, or deepen your sense of intimacy. Others are more of a one-shot exercise and are exploratory in nature.

As you work through the pages of this book, make it your own. Don't get too hung up on following the rules. If a particular exercise leads you down a more intriguing path, take it. Some of these exercises may simply serve as springboards to discussions that fit your style more appropriately. However, if an exercise seems a bit challenging, don't give up on it. As the saying goes, anything worth having is worth working for. In any case, the goal of this workbook is not simply to fortify your reading of *Saving Your Second Marriage Before It Starts* — the goal is to apply it, to make it real.

The Remarriage Motivation Test

On a scale of 1 to 10, rate how much of a factor each of the following motivators are for you to get married. Take time to consider each item, and be as honest as possible.

1. Love at first sight is a factor in why I'm ready to get married again.

Not at All True   Extremely True of Me
1   2   3   4   5   6   7   8   9   10

2. Rebounding from the pain of a previous marriage is a factor in my motivation for this second marriage.

Not at All True   Extremely True of Me
1   2   3   4   5   6   7   8   9   10

3. Rebellion against my ex-husband is a factor in my motivation.

Not at All True   Extremely True of Me
1   2   3   4   5   6   7   8   9   10

4. Loneliness contributes to my reasons for getting married again.

Not at All True   Extremely True of Me
1   2   3   4   5   6   7   8   9   10

5. A sense of obligation is a factor in motivating me to marry.

Not at All True   Extremely True of Me
1   2   3   4   5   6   7   8   9   10

6. Financial advancement is a part of my decision to get remarried.

Not at All True   Extremely True of Me
1   2   3   4   5   6   7   8   9   10

7. Sexual attraction is a factor driving me to get married at this time.

Not at All True   Extremely True of Me
1   2   3   4   5   6   7   8   9   10

8. Escape from an unhappy first marriage is causing me to want to get married again.

Not at All True   Extremely True of Me

1   2   3   4   5   6   7   8   9   10

9. Pressure from others has something to do with why I am getting married again.

Not at All True   Extremely True of Me

1   2   3   4   5   6   7   8   9   10

Scoring: Add up your score from each of the nine items. There are ninety possible points on this test. Add ten to your score. If your score is fifty or less, you can rest easy in the fact that you are probably not getting remarried for some of the most common negative reasons. If your score is greater than twenty-five, you will certainly want to do some soul-searching on your own and with your partner about the items that you ranked highest. We also strongly suggest talking about these motivators with an objective counselor.

The Remarriage Readiness Questionnaire

The following questions will help you assess your readiness for remarriage. Be ruthlessly honest with yourself while answering these questions.

1. Do you know who you are and do you like who you are?

2. Would you say you generally have a healthy sense of self-esteem and confidence?

3. Do you feel comfortable talking about your differences in times of conflict (rather than ignoring them)?

4. Are you twenty years of age or older?

5. Are you twenty-four years of age or older?

6. Would people you respect say you are personally mature?

7. Would you say you have resolved most of the ugly issues with your former husband?

8. Do you feel comfortable thinking for yourself and making your own decisions?

9. Are you able to make decisions without feeling compelled to please others?

10. Are you genuinely prepared to make your marriage relationship of utmost priority?

11. Have you resolved painful or other troubling issues with your past that are bound to impact your new marriage?

12. Have you identified specific quirks or qualities you may be bringing into your marriage as a result of your previous relationship?

13. Have you dated your partner for a year or more?

14. Have you dated your partner for two years or more?

15. Are you willing to take your time in determining whether your relationship is really ready for marriage?

16. Would you characterize your relationship as stable and steadfast?

17. Do you both practice compromise and negotiation effectively in your relationship?

18. Can you both resolve conflict between you without losing control?

19. Are you 100 percent committed, beyond a shadow of a doubt, to making this relationship work?

20. Do you fully agree with your partner's important goals and values?

21. Do you and your partner share many similarities (e.g., sense of humor, habits, goals)?

22. Are your differences tiny compared to your similarities?

23. Do you and your partner have similar family backgrounds?

24. Do you and your partner refrain from criticizing, correcting, or trying to "fix" each other?

25. Do you like this person as he is at this moment (as compared to expecting him to change)?

Scoring: Add up the number of yes responses from these items and multiply by four. That will give you a possible score of 100. If you answered honestly and your score is 90 or higher, your answers indicate you are probably ready for remarriage. A score of 80 to 89 indicates that you are on your way but would probably be wise to give it more time and careful counsel. A score of 79 or lower indicates that you still have a great deal of work to do before you are ready for remarriage. You are likely to benefit from the help of a good counselor and more time. Whether your score is high or low, this brief self-report assessment should serve simply as a guideline, not as the final answer.

Your Personal Ten Commandments

This exercise is designed to help you uncover some of your unspoken rules. It will take about fifteen to twenty minutes.

Try to articulate some of the unspoken rules you grew up with. Take your time to think it over. These unspoken rules are generally so ingrained that we are rarely aware of them.

Once both of you have articulated your "personal ten commandments," share them with each other. Are there rules you would like to change? Take a moment to discuss how unspoken rules might affect your marriage.

1. _____

_____

2. _____

_____

3. _____

_____

4. _____

_____

5. _____

_____

6. _____

_____

7. _____

_____

8. _____

_____

9. _____

_____

10. _____

_____

Anytime you have a fight or disagreement, ask yourself: "Is this fight a result of one of us breaking an unspoken rule?" If so, add that rule to your list, and discuss with your husband how you will handle that situation in the future.

EXERCISE FOUR
Making Your Roles Conscious

Listed below are a number of chores or life tasks that will need to be handled by you or your husband. To make your unconscious understanding of roles conscious, first indicate how your parents handled these tasks. Then write down how you would like to divide up the tasks, according to your understanding of your own and your husband's interests, time, and abilities. Finally, compare your list with your husband's list and discuss the results. Put your final decision of who will do what in the last column, and be prepared to renegotiate when your circumstances change. This exercise will take about thirty minutes.

	Your Mother	Your Father	Both Parents	You	Your Spouse	Both of You	Final Decision
Providing income	❐	❐	❐	❐	❐	❐	_____
Staying home with children	❐	❐	❐	❐	❐	❐	_____
Handling finances	❐	❐	❐	❐	❐	❐	_____
Yard work	❐	❐	❐	❐	❐	❐	_____
Automobile care	❐	❐	❐	❐	❐	❐	_____
Laundry	❐	❐	❐	❐	❐	❐	_____
Dishes	❐	❐	❐	❐	❐	❐	_____
Cleaning	❐	❐	❐	❐	❐	❐	_____
Cooking and baking	❐	❐	❐	❐	❐	❐	_____
Grocery shopping	❐	❐	❐	❐	❐	❐	_____
Caring for pet	❐	❐	❐	❐	❐	❐	_____
Scheduling social events	❐	❐	❐	❐	❐	❐	_____
Maintaining ties with friends and relatives	❐	❐	❐	❐	❐	❐	_____
Planning vacations	❐	❐	❐	❐	❐	❐	_____
Initiating sex	❐	❐	❐	❐	❐	❐	_____
Decorating the house	❐	❐	❐	❐	❐	❐	_____

	Your Mother	Your Father	Both Parents	You	Your Spouse	Both of You	Final Decision
Making major decisions	❏	❏	❏	❏	❏	❏	_____
Initiating discussion about the relationship	❏	❏	❏	❏	❏	❏	_____
Keeping the house neat and orderly	❏	❏	❏	❏	❏	❏	_____
Disciplining the children	❏	❏	❏	❏	❏	❏	_____
Shopping for other needs	❏	❏	❏	❏	❏	❏	_____
Other	❏	❏	❏	❏	❏	❏	_____
Other	❏	❏	❏	❏	❏	❏	_____

Note: We believe that some of these tasks (such as disciplining children or initiating sex) must be shared in order for the couple to have a strong relationship, but in reality many of the tasks may fall disproportionately to the husband or the wife because of unspoken assumptions or circumstances. Use this list periodically to discuss how you are doing and readjust your roles or assignments if you need to.

From Idealizing to Realizing Your Partner

This exercise is designed to help you relinquish unrealistic ideals you might hold of your husband and to discover his true character. It will take about twenty-five to thirty minutes.

Begin by ranking on a one-to-seven scale how much the following traits describe you and your husband. Complete the first two columns ("Your Ranking of You" and then "Your Ranking of Your Husband"). Don't worry about the other two columns just yet.

Your Ranking of You		Your Ranking of Your Husband		Your Husband's Actual Rank		The Difference
___	compassionate	___	-	___	=	___
___	patient	___	-	___	=	___
___	secure	___	-	___	=	___
___	nurturing	___	-	___	=	___
___	insightful	___	-	___	=	___
___	confident	___	-	___	=	___
___	relaxed	___	-	___	=	___
___	tender	___	-	___	=	___
___	even tempered	___	-	___	=	___
___	honest	___	-	___	=	___
___	healthy	___	-	___	=	___
___	spiritual	___	-	___	=	___
___	consistent	___	-	___	=	___

Once you have ranked the first two columns, share your rankings with each other and write them on your own page. Then subtract your husband's actual ranking of himself from your ranking of him. Note any significant differences and discuss them.

One of the central tasks of the early marriage years is to move from "idealizing" your husband to "realizing" your husband. How accurate is your image of who your husband is compared to who he really is? The more accurately you can present yourselves to each other, the easier your first years of marriage will be.

Exercise Six

Exploring Unfinished Business

Marriage is not a quick fix for avoiding your own personal problems. In fact, marriage may even intensify those problems. This exercise is designed to help you honestly face the psychological and spiritual work you need to do as a person so that you do not look to your husband to fulfill needs that he cannot fulfill. It will take about twenty to thirty minutes.

Everyone has yearnings that were seldom if ever fulfilled in their relationship with their parents. Take a moment to reflect, and then write down some of the needs and desires you felt that were never really fulfilled by your parents or by your first husband.

_____

_____

_____

_____

_____

_____

_____

_____

_____

_____

_____

_____

_____

_____

_____

_____

_____

When we marry, we long to recreate the love and closeness and nurturance that we experienced or wished we had experienced in our relationship with our parents. But marriage is not always the place for those yearnings to be fulfilled. No human can meet another person's every need; deep relational longings are ultimately met only in a relationship with God.

If you are willing, share your writing with your husband and discuss the baggage you are both bringing into your marriage.

Assessing Your Self-Image

This exercise is designed to help you measure your self-image and construct an interdependent relationship with your husband. It will take about twenty to thirty minutes.

"You cannot love another person unless you love yourself." Most of us have heard that statement so often we tend to dismiss it as just another catchphrase in the lexicon of pop psychology. But a solid sense of self-esteem is a vital element in building the capacity to love.

The following self-test can give you a quick evaluation of your self-esteem. Answer each with "yes," "usually," "seldom," or "no."

1. Do you believe strongly in certain values and principles, so that you are willing to defend them?

   ❏ Yes   ❏ Usually   ❏ Seldom   ❏ No

2. Do you act on your own best judgment, without regretting your actions if others disapprove?

   ❏ Yes   ❏ Usually   ❏ Seldom   ❏ No

3. Do you avoid worrying about what is coming tomorrow or fussing over yesterday's or today's mistakes?

   ❏ Yes   ❏ Usually   ❏ Seldom   ❏ No

4. Do you have confidence in your general ability to deal with problems, even in the face of failures and setbacks?

   ❏ Yes   ❏ Usually   ❏ Seldom   ❏ No

5. Do you feel generally equal—neither inferior nor superior—to others?

   ❏ Yes   ❏ Usually   ❏ Seldom   ❏ No

6. Do you take it more or less for granted that other people are interested in you and value you?

   ❏ Yes   ❏ Usually   ❏ Seldom   ❏ No

7. Do you accept praise without pretense or false modesty, and accept compliments without feeling guilty?

  ❏ Yes ❏ Usually ❏ Seldom ❏ No

8. Do you resist the efforts of others to dominate you, especially your peers?

  ❏ Yes ❏ Usually ❏ Seldom ❏ No

9. Do you accept the idea—and admit to others—that you are capable of feeling a wide range of impulses and desires, ranging from anger to love, sadness to happiness, resentment to acceptance? (It does not follow, however, that you will act on all these feelings and desires.)

  ❏ Yes ❏ Usually ❏ Seldom ❏ No

10. Do you genuinely enjoy yourself in a wide range of activities, including work, play, creative self-expression, companionship, and just plain loafing?

  ❏ Yes ❏ Usually ❏ Seldom ❏ No

11. Do you sense and consider the needs of others?

  ❏ Yes ❏ Usually ❏ Seldom ❏ No

If your answer to most of the questions are "yes" or "usually," you probably have high self-esteem. If most of your answers were "no" or "seldom," you may likely suffer from a low self-image and thus will need to strengthen it to build the best marriage. Research indicates that self-esteem has a lot to do with the way you will respond to your husband. People with a healthy self-image are more apt to express their opinions, are less sensitive to criticism, and are generally less preoccupied with themselves.

EXERCISE EIGHT
Defining Love

This exercise will help you define love in your own terms and compare your definition with your husband's. It will take fifteen to twenty minutes.

Researcher Beverly Fehr asked more than 170 people to rate the central features of love. The twelve most important attributes they identified are listed below. Take a moment to prioritize this list for yourself.

___ acceptance

___ caring

___ commitment

___ concern for the other's well-being

___ friendship

___ honesty

___ interest in the other

___ loyalty

___ respect

___ supportiveness

___ trust

___ wanting to be with the other

Next, circle your top three attributes of love and write a definition of love that incorporates them.

Love is . . .

_____

_____

_____

_____

_____

_____

_____

_____

_____

_____

Now compare your priorities and your definition with your husband's to see what differences, if any, you might have when it comes to defining love. How has your definition of love changed since your first marriage?

Your Changing Love Style

This exercise will help you understand how love is not stagnant and how the love you have for each other will change during different life passages. It will take twenty-five to thirty minutes.

Using the triangular model of love described in chapter 2 (passion, intimacy, and commitment), draw how your love style with your husband has changed over time. You may want to divide your relationship into three phases and then draw the love triangle that best suits each phase.

As we grow and develop, each stage of the life cycle is marked by the emergence of a new form of love. This means that during certain phases of life, some sides of the triangle will get more attention than others. Using the triangular model of love, draw how your love might look in future passages of marriage, especially if you are blending children into your second marriage.

Discuss with your husband how you feel about the inevitability of love taking on different forms in your future.

Cultivating Intimacy

This exercise will help you open your heart and increase your level of intimacy. It will take about sixty minutes.

Begin by writing about your shared experiences. What is it about your backgrounds that draws you together? What things set the two of you apart from others? What experiences have you had together that bring back fond memories?

_____

_____

_____

_____

_____

_____

_____

_____

Next, focus on things that the two of you share. Begin by jotting down one or two things in each of the following categories, then discuss them with your husband. The more detailed you can be, the better.

- Interests we have in common include:

_____

_____

_____

- Plans we share for our future include:

_____

_____

_____

- Fears and anxieties we both have include:

_____

_____

_____

- Hopes and dreams we share include:

_____

_____

_____

- Spiritual beliefs we both have include:

_____

_____

_____

Conclude this exercise by talking in specific terms about what the two of you can do to cultivate more emotional intimacy in your relationship.

Exercise Eleven
Listening to Your Self-Talk

This exercise will help you and your husband examine how much your attitude shapes the moods of your marriage. It will take about ten to fifteen minutes.

List three circumstances that typically get you into a rotten mood. For example: being stuck in traffic, waiting for someone to arrive who is late, having your credit card rejected, and so on.

1. _____

2. _____

3. _____

There is a maxim in psychology that says "you feel what you think." In other words, your feelings are the result of what is going on in your mind. For each of the bad circumstances you listed above, write down what you are saying to yourself that makes you feel so rotten. For example: "I could be playing tennis instead of being stuck on this freeway."

1. _____

2. _____

3. _____

Now, exercise your power to choose your own attitude by changing your self-talk. Write three alternative statements that would not lead to feeling so rotten. For example: "At least I can use this time to just relax and mentally rehearse my tennis serve."

1. _____

2. _____

3. _____

Negative self-talk can also affect our response to more serious situations. To see how negative self-talk may have affected you, list two situations in your life that were difficult or painful to deal with. For example: losing a job, going through a divorce, or going through a serious illness.

1. _____

2. _____

For each of the crises you listed above, write down things you said to yourself that added to your pain. For example: "I was fired from my job because I'm a natural-born loser."

1. _____

_____

2. _____

_____

Again, exercise your power to choose your own attitude by changing your self-talk. Write two alternative statements that did help or could have helped you adapt to the situation and grow through it. For example: "I will learn from my mistakes and, with God's help, make sure they don't happen again."

1. _____

_____

2. _____

_____

Talk about this exercise with your husband. Discuss how changing your self-talk can improve your chances for marital happiness. How can the two of you team up to fight negative self-talk?

EXERCISE TWELVE
Avoiding the Blame Game

This exercise will help you and your husband take responsibility for your own attitudes. It will take about ten to fifteen minutes.

Below are several scenarios where blame typically enters the picture. For each scenario, decide on your own who is to blame.

First Scene

It's Valentine's Day. Mary has prepared a special meal for Dan—all his favorite foods. She also made him a special Valentine. Dan, however, didn't get Mary anything. After dinner, Dan thanks Mary for the food and slumps into a chair in front of the television. Mary, feeling hurt, leaves the dirty dishes in the sink and goes into the bedroom to cry. Dan realizes what just happened, follows her into the bedroom, and the two accuse each other of being insensitive. Who is at fault?

```
      Dan is to blame          Mary is to blame
   | | | | | | | | | | |
```

Second Scene

Aaron and Kim are having dinner with another couple. During the casual conversation, Kim jokingly makes fun of Aaron's shirt. He laughs at first, but soon he becomes withdrawn, and the conversation becomes noticeably strained. When they get home, both of them accuse the other of ruining the evening. Who is at fault?

```
      Aaron is to blame        Kim is to blame
   | | | | | | | | | | |
```

Third Scene

On a whim, Carl buys a new CD player on sale. He and Michelle had talked about getting one, but they'd decided to wait another year. Carl, however, felt the bargain was too good to pass up and also thought it would be a nice surprise for Michelle. It wasn't. All Michelle could think about was how they were saving money for plane tickets to see her family at Christmas. Carl and Michelle blamed each other for being too controlling with their money. Who is at fault?

Carl is to blame   Michelle is to blame

You may now compare your answers with each other, but there are no "correct" responses. It doesn't matter who is to blame. It doesn't matter who is at fault. What matters in building a happy marriage is defining what the problem is and seeing how each of you can be a part of the solution. Take time to read through the scenarios again, placing yourselves in the couple's shoes. What could each of you do to avoid playing the blame game in these instances?

_____

_____

_____

_____

_____

_____

_____

_____

Adjusting to Things Beyond Your Control

This exercise will help you and your husband more effectively adjust to the jolts of life. It will take about ten to fifteen minutes.

The book talked about how different the Christmas story would be if Mary and Joseph had not had the capacity to adjust to circumstances beyond their control. What situations or circumstances in your wedding and marriage have already thrown you for a loop? Jot down two or three particular challenges you did not anticipate:

_____

_____

_____

_____

_____

How did you respond to these unexpected situations? List some things you did to keep your chin up and some things you did that didn't work as well.

Positive Ways I Coped	Negative Ways I Coped
_____	_____
_____	_____
_____	_____
_____	_____
_____	_____

Now compare your coping strategies with your husband's. In what ways can the two of you improve your capacities to adjust? How can you be better equipped to maintain a positive outlook when similar unexpected circumstances arise in the future?

Conclude this exercise by discussing what will happen in your marriage if you do not practice your ability to adjust to things beyond your control.

How Well Do You Communicate?

This self-test is designed to help you assess how well you communicate with your husband. It will take about ten minutes. Answer the questions as honestly as you can. The more honest you are the more meaningful the exercise will be.

1. The anniversary of your first date is coming up. You have always remembered it and it is important to you, but your husband often forgets, so you:
   A. Wait to see if he'll remember.
   B. Drop hints.
   C. Remind him.

2. If you have a problem with your husband, with whom will you first discuss it?
   A. No one
   B. A friend or close relative
   C. Him

3. He really hurt your feelings. Do you:
   A. Tell him so?
   B. Give him the cold shoulder for a while?
   C. Lash out and hurt him back?

4. If something terribly embarrassing happened to you, would you tell your husband about it?
   A. No
   B. Maybe
   C. Probably

5. Baseball bores you to death, but your husband could discuss it for hours. When the subject comes up, you:
   A. Explain how bored you are and ask him to talk about something else.
   B. Change the subject as soon as possible.
   C. Work on showing some interest.

6. You had an unsuccessful job interview at lunchtime, and you're very upset. When you see your husband later that evening, he looks downcast. You:
   A. Wait until he's in a better mood to tell him about it.
   B. Tell him you didn't get the job but try to hide your emotional reaction.
   C. Begin pouring out your story the moment you see him.

7. For the second time this month your husband has broken a promise to take you to a play. Do you:
   A. Break a promise you've made to see how he likes it?
   B. Sulk and tell him how inconsiderate he is?
   C. Adjust to the letdown but tell him you are annoyed?

Scoring: For one, two, four, five, and seven, give yourself one point for each "A" answer, two for each "B," and three for each "C." Then on questions three and six give yourself three points for each "A," two for each "B," and one for every "C."

7 to 11 points: You need some help in learning how to communicate more effectively. You may have a tendency to become defensive and impatient. Chapter 6 will show you how to improve your skills.

12 to 17 points: You are not doing bad, but there are some sensitive spots in your makeup that tend to block communication. You can really benefit from practicing some of the skills discussed in chapter 6.

18 to 21 points: You're doing quite well in the area of communication, but there's always room for improvement. Chapter 6 will help you fine-tune some skills you are already good at.

The Daily Temperature Reading

This exercise will help you and your husband maintain an easy flow of communication about the big and little things going on in your lives. It will take about thirty minutes.

At first this exercise may seem artificial and even hokey. But in time you'll evolve your own style and find that it is invaluable for staying close. Do it daily, perhaps during a meal. Here are the basics. Sit close, holding each other's hands (touch creates an atmosphere of acceptance), then follow these five steps:

1. *Appreciation.* Take turns expressing appreciation for something your spouse has done. Thank each other.

2. *New Information.* In the absence of information, assumptions (often false ones) rush in. Tell your spouse something new ("We finally got a new account executive at work."). Let your spouse in on your life. And then listen to the news your spouse shares.

3. *Puzzles.* Take turns asking each other something you don't understand but your spouse can explain: "Why were you so down last night?" Or voice a concern about yourself: "I don't know why I got so angry while I was balancing the checkbook yesterday."

4. *Complaint with Request.* Without being judgmental, cite a specific behavior that bothers you and state the behavior you are asking for instead. "When you clean the top of the stove, please dry it with a paper towel. If you don't, it leaves streaks."

5. *Hopes*. Share your hopes, from the mundane ("I hope we have sunshine this weekend.") to the grandiose ("I'd really love to spend a month in Europe with you.").

These simple steps have worked for many couples who want to keep the channels of communication open.

I Can Hear Clearly Now

Your husband will often hide important feelings behind his words. Reflecting his feelings is one of the most helpful and diffcult listening techniques to implement. Following are some statements that a husband might make. Read each separately, listening for feelings. Make note of the feeling you hear and write out a response which reflects that feeling for each of the statements.

1. "I can't believe you agreed to go on this deal tonight without asking me first."

   _____

2. "Can't I relax a minute before we head out again?"

   _____

3. "Why can't you get ready at the same time I do? It seems like I'm always waiting on you."

   _____

4. "Everyone at work seems to be moving up but me."

   _____

5. "What's the use? I can't seem to get through to him, so why try?"

   _____

Now compare your list of reflective statements to those listed on the next page to see how accurately you recognized feelings. Give yourself a 2 on those items where your choice closely matches, a 1 on items where your choice only partially matches, and a 0 if you missed altogether.

Possible Reponses to the Exercise in Active Listening:

1. "Sounds like you are feeling betrayed."
2. "Sounds like you need some time to calm down and recover."
3. "You sound frustrated. I appreciate your patience."
4. "You must feel like you're getting passed over."
5. "Sounds like you're giving up hope."

How you rate on recognizing feelings:

8–10   Above average recognition of feelings

5–7   Average recognition of feelings

0–4   Below average recognition of feelings

Couple's Inventory

This exercise will help you take stock of the roles you both play, consciously and unconsciously, in your relationship. It will take about twenty to thirty minutes.

Complete the following sentences as honestly as you can.

1. I am important to our marriage because

   _____

2. What I contribute to my husband's success is

   _____

3. I feel central to our relationship when

   _____

4. I feel peripheral to our relationship when

   _____

5. The ways I have fun with you are

   _____

6. The way I get space for myself in our relationship is

   _____

7. The ways I am intimate with you are

   _____

8. The role I play as your wife is

   _____

9. I feel most feminine in our relationship when

_____

10. I deal with stress by

_____

11. The division of labor in household tasks is decided by

_____

12. Our finances are controlled by

_____

13. How we spend our spare time is determined by

_____

14. Our social life is planned by

_____

15. I need you to

_____

Compare your statements with each other and discuss how your gender influences the way you responded.

Your Top Ten Needs

This exercise will help you identify some of your deepest needs in a marriage relationship and communicate those needs to your husband. It will take about twenty to thirty minutes.

Listed below are some of the most common needs that people identify as being important in marriage. Rate how important each of these items is for you. If you wish to add other items not included in our list, please do so. As always, do this on your own before discussing it with your husband.

	Not that important						Very important
Admiration	1	2	3	4	5	6	7
Affection	1	2	3	4	5	6	7
Commitment	1	2	3	4	5	6	7
Companionship	1	2	3	4	5	6	7
Conversation	1	2	3	4	5	6	7
Financial support	1	2	3	4	5	6	7
Honesty	1	2	3	4	5	6	7
Intimacy	1	2	3	4	5	6	7
Personal space	1	2	3	4	5	6	7
Respect	1	2	3	4	5	6	7
Rootedness	1	2	3	4	5	6	7
Security	1	2	3	4	5	6	7
Sex	1	2	3	4	5	6	7
Shared Activities	1	2	3	4	5	6	7
_____	1	2	3	4	5	6	7
_____	1	2	3	4	5	6	7

Now that you have completed your list, rank them in order of importance. Next, share the results with your husband. What needs do both of you identify as important? Discuss what needs are most important to you personally. As you discuss them, explain what that need means to you. Men and women often mean different things even when they use the same word (e.g., intimacy). Finally, discuss how each of your needs might change as you grow in marriage.

Exercise Nineteen
Identifying Your Hot Topics

This exercise will help you put your finger on those issues that are especially prone to cause conflict in your relationship. It will take about twenty minutes.

Listed below are the common relationship issues that most couples will encounter from time to time over the course of the relationship. Rate how much of a problem each issue is for you right now. If you wish to add other areas not included in our list, please do so. As always, do this on your own before discussing it with your husband.

	Not at all a problem						*Very much a problem*
Careers	1	2	3	4	5	6	7
Children	1	2	3	4	5	6	7
Chores	1	2	3	4	5	6	7
Communication	1	2	3	4	5	6	7
Friends	1	2	3	4	5	6	7
Illness	1	2	3	4	5	6	7
In-laws	1	2	3	4	5	6	7
Jealousy	1	2	3	4	5	6	7
Money	1	2	3	4	5	6	7
Priorities	1	2	3	4	5	6	7
Recreation	1	2	3	4	5	6	7
Relatives	1	2	3	4	5	6	7
Religion	1	2	3	4	5	6	7
Sex	1	2	3	4	5	6	7

Sleep habits	1	2	3	4	5	6	7
His Ex-wife	1	2	3	4	5	6	7
My Ex-husband	1	2	3	4	5	6	7
_____	1	2	3	4	5	6	7
_____	1	2	3	4	5	6	7

Now that you have completed your list, share the results with your husband. What issues are "hot" for both of you, and what issues are "hot" for one or the other of you? Next, discuss what issues might become more troublesome in the future and what you can do to calm the conflict before it erupts.

Mind Reading

This exercise will help you bring true and false assumptions you are making about your husband into the open so there are fewer surprises and conflicts. It will take about ten minutes.

The next time you sense that your husband is upset with you, pause for a moment and say, "I want to read your mind." Then tell him what you think he was saying to himself. For example, "I think you are mad about the way I left the bed this morning," or "I think you are upset because I wanted to watch TV instead of take a walk." Then say, "How accurate am I?" Your husband can then rate how accurate you are on a percentage scale. For example, he might say, "That's about twenty percent accurate" or "That's one hundred percent accurate."

This simple exercise can be done anytime you sense that your husband is upset and you'd like to know if you are right about the reasons for it. Every couple mind reads every day. This exercise just makes that habit upfront and more useful.

Sharing Withholds

This exercise will help you and your husband keep a clean emotional slate and avoid needless conflicts. We call it "sharing withholds" because it gives couples the chance to share thoughts and feelings that they have withheld from each other. It will take about ten to fifteen minutes.

Begin by writing two things your husband has done in the last forty-eight hours that you sincerely appreciated but did not tell him. For example, "I appreciate the compliment you gave me as I got out of the car yesterday" or "I appreciate the help you gave me in writing my proposal last night."

I appreciate ... _____

I appreciate ... _____

Next, write one thing your husband has done in the last forty-eight hours that irritated you but you did not say anything about. For example, "I didn't like it when you borrowed my umbrella without telling me" or "I didn't like it when you said nothing about the meal I prepared for us last night."

I didn't like it when ... _____

Once both of you have written your statements, take turns sharing them. One person shares all three statements one after the other. Then the other person shares his or her three statements. And here is an important part of this exercise. The person on the receiving end can say only "thank you" after each statement. That's all. Just "thank you." This rule allows couples to share something that bugs them without fearing a blow-up or a defensive reaction. It also allows couples to receive critiques in the context of affirmation.

This exercise can be done every day. Once you get the hang of it, you don't need to write your statements down. All it takes is for one of you to say, "Do you want to share withholds?" Then each of you can take a moment to gather your thoughts, and away you go. Sharing withholds can save you hundreds of hours of needless bickering.

Exercise Twenty-Two
Creating a Clean Slate

To paraphrase Ivy Baker Priest, the end may also be the beginning—if you start again with a clean slate. So if you are entering marriage for the second time, we want to help you do that through this workbook exercise.

Write a short history of your former relationship by completing the following sentence stems:

1. The things that initially attracted me to my first husband were . . .

   _____

2. I decided to marry my first husband because . . .

   _____

3. My first husband contributed to making our marriage work by . . .

   _____

4. I personally contributed to the relationship's difficulties by . . .

   _____

5. I still feel angry about . . .

   _____

6. I still feel guilty about . . .

   _____

7. I still feel sad about . . .

   _____

8. A lesson I've learned about marriage that I'll apply in my second marriage is . . .

_____

9. What my first marriage taught me about myself is . . .

_____

Once you have taken the time to seriously contemplate and respond to each of these items, set aside some meaningful time to discuss them with your partner. If he has been married before, you can take turns responding to each of these items.

Remarried with Children

So you are about to plunge into a new marriage that comes prepackaged with children. Are you ready? Most people would say you're not fully equipped until you've devised a plan. In this exercise we offer a way to get you started in doing just that.

Below is a list of important pointers for building a successful combined family. Read through the list and rank the top half-dozen items you feel are most important for you. It is important to do this on your own at first without influence from your partner.

- Start out in our own new place. This will eliminate turf squabbles, alleviate hurt feelings, and allow us to rid ourselves of the ghosts of the past.
- Ease into the relationships with our children and let them develop gradually. Relationships do not develop on demand. Trust takes time.
- Develop our own new traditions as a family. These will hasten our sense of belonging and connectedness as we develop familiar routines and special celebrations.
- Negotiate differences instead of fighting over right and wrong. Whether we let the dog sleep at the foot of the bed or in the garage is not a matter of right or wrong but simply a difference in preference.
- Maintain a special, planned, one-on-one time that allows our relationship to grow and be nourished in the midst of learning to parent together.
- Support our children's access to both biological parents. We do not want our children to be caught in the middle, nor do we want them to be emotionally torn apart.
- Adults in both households will make direct contact with each other to work out residential schedules with input from the children. We will not talk to each other through the children.
- We understand that much of a child's anger comes from changes and losses they have not chosen. Sharing a parent, a

room, or toy with stepsiblings; going to a new school; missing your other parent, friends, and former neighborhood; having unfamiliar food; adjusting to new rules—all make for some guaranteed difficulties that we will work to understand.

- We will do all we can to learn about the dynamics of stepfamily situations. We will read books, talk to other stepparents, and attend seminars that will sharpen our skills as we work together as a parental team.

- Biological parents and ex-spouses will strive to be cooperative coparents with one another. We will compartmentalize our anger and hurt so we can cooperate on issues regarding the children's well-being. We know that if our conflict continues, the children will suffer.

Once you have ranked your items, compare notes with your partner. Discuss the items each of you checked and explain why. Then use these items to devise a plan for building your combined family together.

EXERCISE TWENTY-FOUR
Your Spiritual Journey

This exercise will help you and your husband share your individual pilgrimages. It will take about fifteen to twenty-five minutes.

Part of cultivating spiritual intimacy comes from merging two individual journeys. We are all beginners when it comes to spiritual development, but each of us has come from different places and traveled different roads to meet where we are today. You may have grown up in a religious home learning Bible verses, going to Sunday school, and studying at a Christian college. Or maybe you never went to church while growing up and are just becoming grounded in your faith. Whatever your story, take a moment to gather your thoughts about your own spiritual quest. Then make a few notes of some of the significant mile markers.

_____

_____

_____

_____

_____

_____

_____

Next, take a moment to complete this brief quiz.

Agree	Disagree	Spouses should ...
❒	❒	pray together every day
❒	❒	study the Bible together regularly
❒	❒	discuss spiritual issues

❏	❏	go to the same church
❏	❏	agree on theology
❏	❏	pay tithe
❏	❏	pray for each other
❏	❏	leave each other's spiritual life up to God
❏	❏	have the same level of spiritual maturity
❏	❏	attend church at least once a week

Once you have gathered your thoughts and completed the quiz, share your journey with your husband. Discuss what has brought you to where you are today. Also, compare how each of you responded to the quiz. Use it as a springboard to a deeper discussion of how each of you views spiritual matters.

EXERCISE TWENTY-FIVE
Improving Your Serve

This exercise will help you and your husband cultivate a soulful marriage by reaching out to others. It will take about ten to fifteen minutes.

Here are a few of the ways couples have practiced the fine art of serving others:

- volunteering in a youth group
- supporting someone's education
- taking care of a shut-in's lawn
- welcoming new people to the neighborhood
- doing short-term relief trips overseas
- sending helpful books to people

Take a moment and list a few ways that you and your husband might reach out together as a team. Work on your own and be as creative as you can:

_____

_____

_____

_____

_____

_____

_____

_____

_____

Now compare your list with your husband's. Combine your lists and begin to rank the items in order of what both of you might like to do as a team. Once you have a couple things that seem like they might fit your joint style, discuss in more detail what they might actually look like. How would the two of you actually live out these forms of service? What do you think reaching out to others might do for your marriage?

EXERCISE TWENTY-SIX
Study Your Spouse

This exercise will help you understand your husband's unique needs now and in the future. It will take about five to ten minutes *each day*.

No one can play as significant a role in encouraging your husband as you. No one can meet his needs better than you. But to be effective, you must study your husband by paying careful attention to his needs, desires, and aspirations.

This exercise is simply a prayer. It need not involve any sharing or discussion with your husband. It simply asks you to study and pray:

God, our Creator, you were there when my husband was formed. You knit him together in his mother's womb. You know his every thought, need, and desire. You are acquainted with all his ways. Enlighten me. Teach me to know this complicated man you have given me to love.

Record your observations below. How does your new understanding of your husband change the way you treat him?

_____

_____

_____

_____

_____

_____

_____

_____

_____

_____

_____

_____

_____

_____

_____

_____

_____

_____

_____

_____

_____

_____

_____

_____

_____

_____

_____

_____

Study your husband. Listen to him, talk to him. And every day, pray this simple prayer, asking God to help you understand him better.

Getting Your Sex Life Off to a Great Start

This exercise is designed to help you dispel some common myths about sex and become more knowledgeable about lovemaking as a married couple.*

Below is a true and false questionnaire for you to complete. Don't worry about getting the right answers. Simply answer each item the best you can.

T F The key to sexual fulfillment is simply to do what comes naturally. In other words, let your instincts be your guide.

T F Most normal married couples have sexual intercourse about two to three times a week.

T F Because men typically have a stronger sex drive than women, it is primarily the husband's job to initiate sex—not the wife's.

T F When it comes down to it, men are almost always ready and willing to have sex, and a good wife should always be available for it.

T F The best way for a woman to have an orgasm is during intercourse.

T F While men have just one orgasm during sex, a woman must have multiple orgasms to be fulfilled sexually.

T F A man's erection is a signal that he is going to need intercourse or ejaculation.

T F The normal position for sexual intercourse is with the man on top.

T F To reach ultimate sexual fulfillment, a couple should strive for simultaneous orgasms, where both the husband and wife climax at the same time.

T F In general, the larger the man's penis, the more pleasurable sex is for the woman.

Number of True answers: _____   Number of False answers: _____

*We are indebted to Cliff and Joyce Penner and Louis and Melissa McBurney for the wealth of knowledge they provide in this area.

Once you have totaled your answers, compare notes and go through the following correct answers together. What matters here is not whether you answered correctly — the point is to learn more accurate information about your sex life as a married couple.

T F   The key to sexual fulfillment is simply to do what comes naturally. In other words, let your instincts be your guide.

While many believe that if you are really good at sex you don't have to learn about it, the truth is that good sex requires much more than just doing what comes naturally. Therefore, one of the best ways to improve your sex life after marriage and to really enjoy it is to educate yourselves, experiment with each other, and teach each other. For example, this may mean reading a book from time to time about sexual intimacy in marriage. The more you learn about sex as a couple, especially each other's preferences and desires, the better your sex life will be. So the answer to this item is false.

T F   Most normal married couples have sexual intercourse about two to three times a week.

When it comes to the frequency of sexual intercourse in your marriage, the two of you determine what is normal. You may have sex twice a day or twice per month. What matters is that, over the course of your married life, you talk about the best balance of your two sexual desires. So the answer to this item is false.

T F   Because men typically have a stronger sex drive than women, it is primarily the husband's job to initiate sex — not the wife's.

Women have sexual urges and thoughts just as men do. In fact, women tend to fantasize even more than men. When women learn to express their sexual urges directly and share their creative fantasies, their husbands are delighted and their sex life is sparked. So it's not up to the man to always initiate sex, and the answer to this item is false. By the way, since women can be more particular about where, when, and how they want to be touched, it takes pressure off the husband and produces greater pleasure for the wife if she also takes the lead.

T F   When it comes down to it, men are almost always ready and willing to have sex, and a good wife should always be available for it.

Yikes! This false belief has led too many couples into trouble because it produces such incredible demand—on both partners. First, it demands that the husband behave as though he is interested even when he is not. And it also demands that the wife be responsive to her husband's arousal even when she is not interested. Truth be told, either one of you can decide to participate in a sexual time together when one of you is feeling the desire and the other is not, but it should not be by demand. Sex should always be a choice. As the Penners say, "Demand is a killer to a healthy, long-term sexual relationship."

T F The best way for a woman to have an orgasm is during intercourse.

Here's the truth: The majority of women do not have orgasms during intercourse. While any woman can learn to be orgasmic during intercourse if she desires to, most women respond orgasmically to manual clitoral stimulation. Of course, some women only respond during intercourse and others respond either way. All variations are delightful ways of receiving sexual pleasure and release, but have nothing to do with "the right way." What is right is what works for you. And keep in mind that the stimulation that triggers the orgasm in the woman has nothing to do with the man or his masculinity. As you both listen to your inner desires and communicate those desires to each other and respond to each other's invitations, the automatic response orgasm is more likely to happen. So the answer to this item is false.

T F While men have just one orgasm during sex, a woman must have multiple orgasms to be fulfilled sexually.

The number of orgasms a woman experiences during sex is not an indicator of her level of sexual fulfillment. Many women are totally satisfied after one release. Others quickly get restimulated and desire more. So, for the man, there's no need to equate the number of orgasms with his level of "performance." So the answer to this item is false.

T F A man's erection is a signal that he is going to need intercourse or ejaculation.

An erection simply means a man is aroused, and that's all. An erection for the man is no different than vaginal lubrication for the woman. It's not a demand for action, even though many men say they just cannot handle getting aroused and not having an ejaculation. The truth is that all men get erections every eighty to ninety minutes while they sleep, but these erections rarely lead to an ejaculation. It is equally possible to allow arousal to come and go during caressing or in response to seeing his wife's body. So, again, the answer to this item is false.

T   F   The normal position for sexual intercourse is with the man on top.

The man-on-top position is commonly used by many couples, but that does not make it the normal or right position. With more sexual experiences together in your marriage, you will discover positions that bring you the most pleasure. You need to feel free to try a variety of positions in your lovemaking. So the answer is false.

T   F   To reach ultimate sexual fulfillment, a couple should strive for simultaneous orgasms, where both the husband and wife climax at the same time.

Having simultaneous orgasms can be fun if it happens, but it's an unnecessary goal to put on your lovemaking. It has absolutely nothing to do with how successful you are as a couple. The demand for both spouses to have orgasms at the same time gets in the way of the pleasure of enjoying each other. Many couples prefer separate orgasms so each one can experience the other's. So, again, the answer is false.

T   F   In general, the larger the man's penis, the more pleasurable sex is for the woman.

Penis size is the source of many myths. But in truth, it has nothing to do with a man's sexuality, his attractiveness to his wife, his skill as a lover, or the satisfaction he can bring to his wife. The quality of sex is not in any way related to penis size. When erect, penises vary little in size from one to another. A smaller, flaccid penis enlarges proportionately more when erect than does a larger flaccid penis. Also, the vagina adapts to the penis, and it is only in the outer third of the vagina that the woman reasons to the penis. The shortest penis is more than adequate to bring pleasure to a woman. So the answer is false. The penis myths perpetuated by locker-room jokes have nothing to do with reality.

So, each of the ten items in this self-test is false. If you answered any of them as true, don't feel badly. Each of these items represents one of the most common myths about marital sex. And now that you know the truth, you are far more likely to get your sex life off to a great start.

Of course, to augment your sexual knowledge, you will also need a solid understanding of the male and female anatomy. You have probably already studied this in school, but even so, it's very helpful to brush up on this information. Cliff and Joyce Penner's bestselling book *The Gift of Sex* is a terrific resource for this, as is Louis and Melissa McBurney's book *Real Questions, Real Answers About Sex*.

But we want to leave you with one more thought. Remember that one of the keys to a great sex life is to talk openly about it as husband and wife. Far too many married couples simply don't discuss their sex life together. Once you are married, we recommend that you talk in specific terms by completing such sentences as:

> I feel sexually aroused by you when . . .
> When we are making love, I really enjoy . . .
> When we are making love, I feel uncomfortable when you . . .
> The surest turnoff for me is . . .
> The surest turn-on for me is . . .
> What you need to know about me when it comes to sex is . . .

These kinds of specific statements will do wonders for your sex life right from the start and ensure "hot monogamy" for decades.

Money Talks and So Can We

This exercise will help you delve into money matters that will impact your marriage in countless ways. It may take a bit longer than some of the other exercises in this workbook, but it is immensely practical and will benefit you for decades.

Your Family and Money

You already know from earlier exercises that your family of origin shapes nearly everything you do. And how you relate to money is not an exception. So let's begin by having you simply note how money was treated, valued, and managed in your home growing up. How did your childhood shape your beliefs about money? Make a few notes here so that you can discuss it in a moment with your partner. Be sure to note how you think you are similar or different than your parents when it comes to money matters. And also note how you see money being managed in your home together.

_____

_____

_____

_____

The Money Self-Test

What follows is a series of statements for you to rate. There are no right or wrong answers, and don't try to answer how you think others might want you to. Be honest. This is a self-test that will help you and your partner get real about personal finances.

1. I feel comfortable talking about finances with my partner.

| Never | Rarely | Sometimes | Often | Always |

2. I pay bills on time.

Never   Rarely   Sometimes   Often   Always

3. I pay off my credit card balance every month.

Never   Rarely   Sometimes   Often   Always

4. I save a portion of my income every month.

Never   Rarely   Sometimes   Often   Always

5. I give a predetermined portion of my money to charities or my church every month.

Never   Rarely   Sometimes   Often   Always

6. I manage my money with a set budget that I follow.

Never   Rarely   Sometimes   Often   Always

7. I buy things on impulse.

Never   Rarely   Sometimes   Often   Always

8. Most people who know me well would say I'm a saver and rather tight with my money.

Never   Rarely   Sometimes   Often   Always

9. I know how much I have in my bank account at almost any given time.

Never   Rarely   Sometimes   Often   Always

10. I regularly keep track of what I spend and where I spend it.

Never   Rarely   Sometimes   Often   Always

11. When it comes to investing, I give serious thought to and study how I can invest my money for high returns in the long run.

Never   Rarely   Sometimes   Often   Always

Once you have completed this self-test, take a few minutes to talk with your partner about money matters. Begin by discussing how your families approached finances. And keep in mind that this discussion is simply about getting money matters on the table. It's not about judging each other's approaches. And as you compare your answers on your two self-tests, note each item where your answers are quite divergent.

Here are a few questions to help you organize your findings:

1. Do you have the same or different views on spending styles, credit, and debt?

_____

_____

2. Your views on giving and saving money and investing for the future?

_____

_____

3. Your views on working with a financial plan and budget?

_____

_____

Do You Clash over Cash?

After this discussion, rank on the following continuum where the two of you might fall when it comes to money matters:

Out of sync   In sync

  1   2   3   4   5   6   7   8   9   10

Don't be disturbed if you find you have many divergent views on finances as a couple. Most couples do. What matters is what you are going to do about it. What follows are practical suggestions to help you begin implementing a proven plan.

If Either One of You Is in Debt, Start Digging Out

If you haven't done so already, each of you needs to be up front with the other about where you are personally on your finances as it relates to debt. We've seen many couples who get married only to discover that their partner has a significant amount of debt that was never disclosed beforehand. Don't allow this to happen to you, and don't hold back this kind of information from your partner. You will wrestle with trust issues for decades as a result of not being up front early on. And it's simple. It basically involves answering three primary questions:

1. Do you have credit card debt? If so, how much?
2. Do you have loans you are paying off? If so, how much?
3. Do you owe anyone money? If so, how much?

Now if either of you has financial debt, you need to devise a plan together for getting out of it as soon as possible. If the debt is significant, this may mean talking with a financial consultant who specializes in these matters. One of the most respected and successful do-it-yourself programs comes from Dave Ramsey, and you can visit his website at *www.daveramsey.com*. You'll want to implement a cash control system, for example, and you will find all the tools you need for this at his site. Digging out of debt is the first order of business in getting on your feet financially as a couple.

Design a Budget

Whether you have debt or not, we strongly recommend that you design a budget together as a couple. Why? Because a budget allows you to control your money rather than the other way around. And it's not as bad as you might imagine. It begins by getting an accurate picture of your total income and then deciding how you will allocate it. Of course, this may be revised as circumstances change, but you've got to start somewhere. Here's a budget worksheet that will help you get going:

Basic Budget Worksheet

CATEGORY	MONTHLY BUDGET AMOUNT	MONTHLY ACTUAL AMOUNT	DIFFERENCE BETWEEN ACTUAL AND BUDGET
INCOME:			
Wages Paid			
Bonuses			
Interest Income			
Capital Gains Income			
Dividend Income			

CATEGORY	MONTHLY BUDGET AMOUNT	MONTHLY ACTUAL AMOUNT	DIFFERENCE BETWEEN ACTUAL AND BUDGET
Miscellaneous Income			
INCOME SUBTOTAL			
EXPENSES:			
Mortgage or Rent			
TV Cable			
Telephone			
Home Repairs/ Maintenance			
Car Payments			
Gasoline/Oil			
Auto Repairs/ Maintenance/Fees			
Other Transportation (tolls, bus, subway, etc.)			
Child Care			
Auto Insurance			
Home Owner's/ Renter's Insurance			
Computer Expense			
Entertainment/ Recreation			
Groceries			
Toiletries, Household Products			
Clothing			
Eating Out			
Gifts/Donations/Tithe			
Health Care (medical/dental/vision, incl. insurance)			

CATEGORY	MONTHLY BUDGET AMOUNT	MONTHLY ACTUAL AMOUNT	DIFFERENCE BETWEEN ACTUAL AND BUDGET
Hobbies			
Interest Expense (mortgage, credit cards, fees)			
Magazines/Newspapers			
Federal Income Tax			
State Income Tax			
Social Security/ Medicare Tax			
Personal Property Tax			
Pets			
Miscellaneous Expenses			
EXPENSES SUBTOTAL			
NET INCOME (INCOME LESS EXPENSES)			

Here's How to Use This Worksheet:

- Go through your checkbook or bills for the last two to three months and add and delete categories from the worksheet to fit your expenditures.
- Think about your hobbies and your habits and be sure to add categories for these expenses.
- Go through your pay stubs and calculate your average monthly gross pay. Do the same for any interest income, dividends, bonuses, or other miscellaneous income.
- For each expense category, try to determine a budget amount that realistically reflects your actual expenses while setting targeted spending levels that will enable you to save money.
- If an expense is incurred more or less often than monthly, convert it to a monthly amount when calculating the monthly budget

amount. For instance, an auto expense that is billed every six months would be converted to monthly by dividing the six month premium by six.

- Once you're comfortable with your expense categories and budgeted amounts, enter expenditures from your checkbook from the last month.
- Keep track of cash expenditures throughout the month and total and categorize these at the end of each month.
- Subtotal the income and expense categories. Subtract the total expenses from the total income to arrive at your net income.
- If the number is negative, your expenses are greater than your income. Your situation can probably be greatly improved by changing your spending habits.
- After you've tracked your actual spending for a month or two, analyze your spending to identify where you can comfortably make cuts.
- Once you've got the budgeting process in place, take an in-depth look at your largest spending categories, brainstorm about ways to reduce spending in specific categories, and set realistic goals.

Keep this in mind: One of the top reasons, if not *the* top reason, so many people fail at budgeting is attitude. If you think of it as a penny-pinching sacrifice instead of a means for achieving your financial goals and dreams, how long are you likely to stick with it? Many people refuse to budget because of budgeting's negative connotation. If you're one of these people, try thinking of it as a "spending plan" instead of a "budget." It's like the difference between going on a diet and eating healthily. One is negative and restrictive; the other is positive and allows you to indulge now and then and still achieve your goals.

Talk about Your Financial Goals

Throughout your marriage you will talk about financial goals from time to time, but this is an important topic at the start as well. So take another moment or two to consider where you and your partner would like to be financially in another year, another five years, ten years, and so on. Here are some questions to generate this discussion:

1. What are your thoughts on owning your own home?
2. Have you considered how your finances will be impacted by having children?
3. Do you have a plan for paying off car loans?
4. What are your goals when it comes to giving money away and supporting causes you believe in?

Sessions

*FOR GROUP OR COUPLE
DISCUSSION WITH
THE DVD CURRICULUM*

Introduction

Studying this material in a group with other couples is one of the best ways to make it stick — and have a lot of fun in the process. To that end, we've created this seven-session group discussion guide. Most people feel this is just about the right length for a group series, plus we've included two additional sessions targeted specifically to those considering remarriage. Though we've created this discussion guide for group use, it is also adaptable for individual couple's study if you and your partner prefer to go through the questions on your own or are unable to connect with others who are studying the same curriculum.

Before your group meetings, it would be helpful for you to read the assigned chapters associated with the session, but this is not required. Obviously, you are going to get more out of the discussion if you've "done your homework." So if you can make the time to read the chapters, great! If not, don't worry. You can still join in on the discussion (it doesn't rely on having read the chapters), and you don't need to feel an ounce of guilt. The purpose is to enjoy the interaction and to learn from it. You can always read the chapters later, if you wish.

Here's a quick glimpse at what you'll be doing in each group session. We've designed each session to last about an hour, but you can take more or less time as your schedule dictates.

Just for Fun (4 minutes)

Each session begins with a question or activity that is "just for fun" — a kind of icebreaker. These are just to get the wheels turning and to help you connect as you come together as a group.

DVD Notes (15 – 20 minutes)

In addition to hearing from Les and Leslie Parrott, each of the seven sessions will include two brief video segments featuring several real-life couples who are exploring these issues just as you are. As you watch the DVD, feel free to fill in the content points supplied, in addition to jotting down your notes, questions, and reactions in the space provided.

Exploring Your Workbook Exercise (15 – 20 minutes)

Each of the sessions will rely on an exercise from this workbook. You will typically spend time within the group session doing the exercise, then discussing it. While of course it would be helpful to have the exercises completed beforehand, you may do them within your group if you wish. We've selected exercises that will not put anyone on the spot or force anyone to share information they don't want to. Of course, your group may elect to use other exercises from this workbook to discuss if you wish. That's up to you and your group.

Time to Discuss (20 minutes)

The list of questions you'll find in this section is designed to spark ideas, reactions, and real-life examples. As you interact, remember that a key ingredient to successful group discussion is vulnerability. This doesn't mean you have to say anything you don't want to. It's just that, typically, the more transparent you are, the more meaningful the experience will be, and the more open others will be as well. Vulnerability begets vulnerability. However, we caution you not to use this time to gripe about your partner in some way. Don't embarrass each other by dragging out dirty laundry you know would upset your partner. You want to be genuine and vulnerable, but not at the expense of your partner's feelings.

Another key ingredient in these discussions is specificity. You'll gain much more out of this time when you use specific examples with each other. So with this in mind, we will remind you to "be specific" every so often.

Finally, if you are a group facilitator, don't feel that you need to follow the order given or even use every question. Let the dynamics of the discussion be your guide.

Taking Time as a Couple

Finally, we've included suggestions for ways you can take this group experience into your week together as a couple. We encourage you to further discuss and apply the material as a way to connect and grow together. And of course you can also read the book together or individually if you can make the time. Again, no pressure or guilt.

One more thing: Relax. Have fun. And enjoy the opportunity to master life skills that will improve your relationship and help you develop a strong foundation for a marriage that will last a lifetime.

Have You Faced the Myths of Marriage with Honesty?

*What you believe about marriage will become
the fuel for your behavior in marriage.
For this reason, exploring the myths of marriage is essential.*

Just for Fun (4 minutes)

Whether you are doing this as an individual couple or as a small group of couples, take a moment to name one of the most romantic movies you've ever seen. It could be *Sleepless in Seattle, Casablanca, Titanic, Jerry Maguire, Father of the Bride, When Harry Met Sally*, or any of the hundreds of other romantic stories. What makes this movie so romantic to you? Do you see yourself in it? From your perspective, what's the primary message of the movie? If you don't like this line of questioning, name a romantic movie that you didn't like. Why?

_____

_____

_____

_____

DVD Segment #1 Notes (13 minutes)

• Your beliefs are the fuel for your behavior.

• Myth #1: _____

• Unspoken Rules

- Unconscious Roles

Exploring Your Workbook Exercise (20 minutes)

Within your small group, take time to complete exercise 4 in your workbook. This exercise explores making conscious your understanding of the roles both you and your partner have in a marriage. If you are comfortable, share with the group: What insights did you have while doing this exercise? How have your families of origin influenced your understanding of roles? What items did you have to renegotiate?

DVD Segment # 2 Notes (8 minutes)

- Myth #2:_____

- Myth #3:_____

- Myth #4:_____

- If you try to build intimacy with another person before getting whole on your own, all your relationships become an attempt to complete yourself.

- A-Frame Relationship =_____

- H-Frame Relationship = _____

- M-Frame Relationship = _____

Time to Discuss (20 minutes)

1. Which ideas expressed in the video were new to you?

_____

_____

_____

_____

_____

2. Which concept talked about in today's session can you apply to your relationship?

_____

_____

_____

_____

3. In what areas of your life is your relationship operating as an **A, H,** or **M**?

_____

_____

_____

_____

_____

4. What other myths do couples bring to the marriage relationship?

_____

_____

_____

_____

_____

Taking Time as a Couple

To further explore marital myths you may have believed, spend some time this week as a couple reading chapter 2 and completing exercises 1, 3, 5, 6, and 7 in the workbook. If you have time, also discuss the reflection questions with your partner.

SESSION TWO
Can You Identify Your Love Style?

Do you have a crystal clear concept of love?
And do you see it the same way as your partner? This session will ensure
that you get on the same page as you write your love story together.

Just for Fun (4 minutes)

Whether you are doing this as an individual couple or as a small group of couples, take a moment to answer these questions together: If you were designing a recipe for the perfect romantic day, and money wasn't an object, what would go into it and why? What would you do together to cultivate romance for twenty-four hours with an unlimited budget? As you reflect on this daydream, consider how romance relates to love. In other words, what percentage of married love do you think involves romance?

_____

_____

_____

_____

DVD Segment #1 Notes (7 minutes)

• Passion is the _____ component of love.

• Intimacy is the _____ component of love.

• Commitment is the _____ component of love.

Exploring Your Workbook Exercise (15 minutes)

Within your small group, take time to complete exercise 8 in your workbook. This exercise should help you define love in your own terms and compare your definition with your partner's. What qualities of love were most important to you? To your partner? Discuss with the group how your definition of love compared to your partner's.

DVD Segment #2 Notes (11 minutes)

• How to cultivate passion (for women): _____

• How to cultivate intimacy (for men): _____

• How to cultivate commitment (for both men and women):

_____

Time to Discuss (20 minutes)

1. Which idea presented in today's session did you find most interesting? Why?

_____

_____

_____

_____

_____

2. In your love life right now, which component of love seems most powerful: passion, intimacy, or commitment? Why?

_____

_____

_____

_____

_____

3. In what ways can you nurture each component of love: passion, intimacy, and commitment?

_____

_____

_____

_____

4. Why is it important to remember that love is constantly changing and growing?

_____

_____

_____

_____

_____

Taking Time as a Couple

In order to better understand your love style, spend some time this week as a couple reading chapter 3 and completing exercises 9 and 10 in the workbook. If you have time, also discuss the reflection questions with your partner.

Have You Developed the Habit of Happiness?

*This habit can make or break a marriage. And it's important to remember
that it has little to do with your partner and everything to do with you.
In other words, an upbeat attitude is highly contagious.*

Just for Fun (4 minutes)

Whether you are doing this as an individual couple or as a small group of couples, take a moment to answer these questions together: Consider a time when you had "one of those days" — a time when nothing seemed to go as planned. Looking back on it, can you find any humor in it? If your experience was written into a sitcom, what would the name of the show be called and why? Now, think about how you typically respond when unexpected circumstances interrupt your plans. Anything you'd like to change about your attitude in these times?

_____

_____

_____

_____

DVD Segment #1 Notes (9 minutes)

• The one habit that can make or break your relationship is the

capacity to _____.

Exploring Your Workbook Exercise (15 minutes)

Within your group, complete exercise 11 in your workbook. Share with others how you see your attitude shaping the moods of your marriage. What types of things affect your mood? What negative self-talk have you used, and how can you help your partner avoid negative self-talk that she might use?

DVD Segment #2 Notes (7 minutes)

- The 3 toxins that can seep into a marriage relationship:

_____

_____

_____

- The most important quality of a marriageable person is

_____.

Time to Discuss (20 minutes)

1. What struck you most about today's session?

_____

_____

_____

_____

_____

2. When are you most likely to blame your partner?

_____

_____

_____

_____

_____

3. Do you think the most important quality of a marriageable person is the habit of happiness? Why or why not?

_____

_____

_____

_____

_____

4. What keeps you from *choosing* to be happy?

_____

_____

_____

_____

_____

Taking Time as a Couple

To further explore how your attitudes can affect your marriage, spend some time this week as a couple reading chapter 4 and completing exercises 12 and 13 in the workbook. If you have time, also discuss the reflection questions with your partner.

Can You Say What You Mean and Understand What You Hear?

Communication is the lifeline of every marriage. But too often the lines of communication between couples get crossed. Rest assured that this session will help you speak each other's language fluently.

Just for Fun (4 minutes)

If you are doing this as a small group of couples, take a moment to play the "whisper" game. One of you begins by whispering something (at least three sentences long)—it can be about anything (what you had for lunch, what you like to do on vacation, your idea of a dream wedding)—and the task is to convey the message around the entire group. You can't ask a person to repeat the message. You simply have to whisper to the next person what you heard. You'll be surprised by how the message ends up. If you are doing this session as an individual couple, talk about a time when you encountered a major miscommunication. What happened?

_____

_____

_____

_____

DVD Segment #1 Notes (10 minutes)

- Men _____ talk

- Women _____ talk

- Communication Basics

- Skill #1:_____

Exploring Your Workbook Exercise (15 minutes)

Within your small group, complete exercise 14 in your workbook. Compare your score with your partner's and discuss how well each of you are communicating. If you are comfortable, share with your group areas in which you can improve your communication.

DVD Segment #2 Notes (7 minutes)

- Communication Basics

- Skill #2:

  _____

- Without being genuine, the best communication techniques in the world will fall flat.

Time to Discuss (20 minutes)

1. Which ideas presented in today's session were new to you?

_____

_____

_____

_____

2. Which concept presented in this session seems most difficult for you to put into practice?

_____

_____

_____

_____

3. Empathy involves using your head _and_ your heart. Which do you tend to use more—your head or your heart? How can you begin to cultivate using both in your interactions with your partner?

_____

_____

_____

_____

4. When do you feel most understood? When do you feel least understood? In what ways can you better communicate your own feelings about being understood?

_____

_____

_____

_____

_____

Taking Time as a Couple

To learn more about successful communication in your marriage, spend some time this week as a couple reading chapter 5 and completing exercises 15 and 16 in the workbook. If you have time, also discuss the reflection questions with your partner.

Have You Bridged the Gender Gap?

Everybody knows that men and women are different. But what most newlywed couples don't realize, until they cross the proverbial threshold, is just how pronounced that difference is. This session will help make that transition much easier.

Just for Fun (10 minutes)

If you are studying this curriculum with other couples, divide into two groups: men in one group and women in another. In each group, appoint a facilitator and a secretary. Answer the question, "What do you want the other gender to know about your gender?" What insights do you gain from hearing what the other group has to say? If you and your partner are completing this on your own, discuss the same question with each other.

_____

_____

_____

_____

DVD Segment #1 Notes (11 minutes)

• How men and women solve problems:

• Men want to _____ it.

• Women want to _____ it.

Exploring Your Workbook Exercise (20 minutes)

Within your group, complete exercise 18. This exercise should help you communicate your deepest needs to your partner. Share with the group the needs that were most important to you. How did these needs compare with those of your partner? How do you see your needs changing as you grow in your marriage?

DVD Segment #2 Notes (7 minutes)

• Men need _____ _____.

• Women need to be _____.

Time to Discuss (20 minutes)

1. What ideas did you hear today that were new to you?

_____

_____

_____

_____

_____

2. What general gender differences have you experienced in your relationship?

_____

_____

_____

_____

_____

3. How can these gender differences cause conflict in your marriage?

_____

_____

_____

_____

_____

4. What steps can you take to celebrate the differences you both bring to your marriage?

_____

_____

_____

_____

_____

Taking Time as a Couple

To further explore how gender differences affect your marriage, spend some time this week as a couple reading chapter 6 and completing exercise 17 in the workbook. If you have time, also discuss the reflection questions with your partner.

Do You Know How to Fight a Good Fight?

Conflict is inevitable. No matter how "in love" a couple is, friction eventually emerges. But the savvy couple knows how to use this conflict to their advantage. This session will show you how.

Just for Fun (4 minutes)

Sometimes people fight about the silliest things—like an insignificant detail in a story they are telling, how someone is driving the car, etc. What's the craziest conflict you have ever heard of and why? Also, have you ever encountered a conflict because you were convinced you were right about something and it turned out you weren't? If so, are you willing to share it?

_____

_____

_____

_____

DVD Segment #1 Notes (12 minutes)

- Negative feelings that get buried have a high rate of resurrection.

Exploring Your Workbook Exercise (15 minutes)

Within your group, complete exercise 21 in the workbook. The skills learned from this exercise should help you and your partner avoid needless conflicts by remaining emotionally open with one another. If you are comfortable, share with the group how you felt when sharing withholds with your partner.

DVD Segment #2 Notes (8 minutes)

• What to avoid in conflict:

_____

_____

_____

_____

• XYZ Formula: In situation X, when you do Y, I feel Z.
• A great way to turn a _____

  into a _____

Time to Discuss (20 minutes)

1. What causes the biggest conflicts in your relationship?

_____

_____

_____

_____

_____

2. How do you usually handle conflict?

_____

_____

_____

_____

_____

3. As you were growing up, how did your family typically handle conflict? What habits have you taken with you into your adult life?

_____

_____

_____

_____

_____

4. What "conflict habits" have you brought to your new relationship?

_____

_____

_____

_____

_____

Taking Time as a Couple

To further explore how to handle conflict in your marriage, spend some time this week as a couple reading chapter 7 and completing exercises 19 and 20 in the workbook. If you have time, also discuss the reflection questions with your partner.

Are You and Your Partner Soul Mates?

You can do everything right in marriage and still wake up one morning and wonder, "Is this it?" You will continually be looking for depth and meaning in your relationship until you explore your spiritual nature — how the two of you walk together with God. This session will show you how to do just that.

Just for Fun (4 minutes)

Research shows that married couples who pray together enjoy a better sex life. What do you think of that? Why do you think this is so? And what does it say to you about the spiritual aspect of a married couple's life together?

_____

_____

_____

_____

DVD Segment #1 Notes (6 minutes)

• On a scale of 1 – 10, most churchgoing couples rate the importance of spiritual intimacy as a 9 or 10, yet rate the level of satisfaction with their spiritual intimacy as a 2 or 3.

• Couples who pray together report higher satisfaction with their sex lives.

Exploring Your Workbook Exercise (15 minutes)

Within your group, complete exercise 25 in your workbook. This exercise explores reaching out to others as a way to strengthen your marriage. What are some activities you and your partner came up with to serve others? How do you think this service will impact your marriage?

DVD Segment #2 Notes (8 minutes)

• When it comes to cultivating spiritual intimacy together, every couple has their own unique style.

Time to Discuss (20 minutes)

1. On a scale of 1 to 10, how important is spiritual intimacy in your marriage? Explain your answer.

_____

_____

_____

_____

_____

2. On that same scale of 1 to 10, how satisfied are you with your current level of spiritual intimacy? Explain your answer.

_____

_____

_____

_____

_____

3. What are you presently doing in the area of shared service?

_____

_____

_____

_____

_____

4. What is one thing you can do as a couple to strengthen the spiritual aspect of your relationship?

_____

_____

_____

_____

_____

Taking Time as a Couple

To further explore the spiritual nature of your marriage, spend some time this week as a couple reading chapter 9 and completing exercises 24 and 26 in the workbook. If you have time, also discuss the reflection questions with your partner.

Additional Sessions

FOR COUPLES CONSIDERING REMARRIAGE

Are You Ready to Get Married Again?

Whether it's one partner or both that are entering a second marriage,
being fully prepared for the unique challenges remarriage presents is essential.
This session will help you explore critical remarriage issues that you'll want to address —
so you are both ready for a relationship that lasts a lifetime.

Just for Fun (4 minutes)

Describe your first impression of each other. What was that first encounter like, and how has your first impression changed from then to now? How has it remained the same?

_____

_____

_____

_____

DVD Notes (13 minutes)

_____

_____

_____

_____

_____

_____

_____

Exploring Your Workbook Exercise (15 minutes)

Within your group, complete exercise 2 in your workbook. Discuss your responses with the group. Remember, there's no need to disclose anything you feel is too personal or private, but share what you learned about yourself and your relationship as a result of completing this exercise.

Time to Discuss (20 minutes)

1. What have you heard about remarriage (from friends, family, media, and so on)?

_____

_____

_____

_____

2. In the video session you just watched, what comments from couples in this session do you most resonate with and why?

_____

_____

_____

_____

3 What does "relational readiness for remarriage" mean to you? How do you know when the relationship is in a good place to move into remarriage?

_____

_____

_____

_____

4. In your opinion, what is likely to be a unique challenge you might face as a couple involved in a remarriage?

_____

_____

_____

_____

Taking Time as a Couple

To further explore whether you are ready for remarriage, spend some time this week as a couple reading chapter 1 and completing exercise 1 in the workbook. If you have time, also discuss the reflection questions with your partner.

Do You Know How to Blend a Family?

If you are marrying for the second time, you already know there are special challenges that are unique to your situation — especially if you are blending a family. This session is specifically for you.

Just for Fun (4 minutes)

Perhaps the modern-day iconic image of a second marriage situation is found in the 1970s sitcom *The Brady Bunch*. Take a moment to talk about this program. What are some of the memories you have from watching this show? And what, if anything, did this show have to say about a second marriage where kids are involved?

_____

_____

_____

_____

DVD Notes (16 minutes)

_____

_____

_____

_____

_____

_____

_____

_____

Exploring Your Workbook Exercise (20 minutes)

Within your group, take time to complete exercise 23 in your workbook. This exercise will help you determine what is most important for you in building a successful combined family. Discuss your responses with your partner before sharing with the group. Remember, there's no need to disclose anything you feel is too personal or private.

Time to Discuss (20 minutes)

1. If you are the biological parent, what is one specific thing you can do to improve the blending process? Is there anything about your personal situation that will make blending your family more difficult?

\
\
\
\
\
\
\

2. Discipline is a big issue in blended families. If you are the biological parent, how can you take some concrete steps to be the primary disciplinarian?

\
\
\
\
\
\

3. If you are a stepparent it can sometimes be tough to give your spouse time alone with his or her biological children. What can you do to feel good about this and ensure that it happens?

_____

_____

_____

_____

_____

4. Consider building new family traditions and activities into your blended family. What might they be? How can you respect the old traditions while building new ones?

_____

_____

_____

_____

_____

Taking Time as a Couple

To further explore the topic of blending a family, take time this week as a couple reading chapter 8 and completing exercise 22 in the workbook.

Saving Your Marriage Before It Starts

Seven Questions to Ask Before—and After— You Marry

Drs. Les and Leslie Parrott

A trusted marriage resource for engaged and newlywed couples is now expanded and updated.

With more than 500,000 copies in print, *Saving Your Marriage Before It Starts* has become the gold standard for helping today's engaged and newlywed couples build a solid foundation for lifelong love. Trusted relationship experts Drs. Les and Leslie Parrott offer seven time-tested questions to help couples debunk the myths of marriage, bridge the gender gap, fight a good fight, and join their spirits for a rock-solid marriage.

This expanded and updated edition of *Saving Your Marriage Before It Starts* has been honed by ten years of feedback, professional experience, research, and insight, making this tried-and-true resource better than ever. Specifically designed to meet the needs of today's couples, this book equips readers for a lifelong marriage before it even starts.

The men's and women's workbooks include self-tests and exercises sure to bring about personal insight and help you apply what you learn. The seven-session DVD features the Parrotts' lively presentation as well as real-life couples, making this a tool you can use "right out of the box." Two additional sessions for second marriages are also included. The unabridged audio CD is read by the authors.

The Curriculum Kit includes DVD with Leader's Guide, hardcover book, workbooks for men and women, and *Saving Your Second Marriage Before It Starts* workbooks for men and women. All components, except for DVD, are also sold separately.

Curriculum Kit   0-310-27180-0

Also Available:

0-310-26210-0	Saving Your Marriage Before It Starts	Audio CD, Unabridged
0-310-26565-7	Saving Your Marriage Before It Starts Workbook for Men	Softcover
0-310-26564-9	Saving Your Marriage Before It Starts Workbook for Women	Softcover
0-310-27585-7	Saving Your Second Marriage Before It Starts Workbook for Women	Softcover
0-310-27584-9	Saving Your Second Marriage Before It Starts Workbook for Men	Softcover

Your Time-Starved Marriage

How to Stay Connected at the Speed of Life

Drs. Les and Leslie Parrott

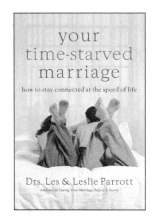

This is not a book about being more productive —it's a book about being more connected as a couple. In *Your Time-Starved Marriage*, Drs. Les and Leslie Parrott show how you can create a more fulfilling relationship with time—and with each other.

The moments you miss together are gone forever. Irreplaceable. And yet, until now, there has not been a single book for couples on how to better manage and reclaim this priceless resource. The Parrotts show you how to take back the time you've been missing together—and maximize the moments you already have. *Your Time-Starved Marriage* shows you how to

- relate to time in a new way as a couple
- understand the two lies every time-starved couple so easily believes
- slay the "busyness" giant that threatens your relationship
- integrate your time-style with a step-by-step approach that helps you make more time together
- stop the "time bandits" that steal your minutes
- maximize mealtime, money time, and leisure time
- reclaim all the free time you've been throwing away

Learn to manage your time together more than it manages you. Dramatically improve your ability to reclaim the moments you've been missing. *Your Time-Starved Marriage* gives you tools to feed your time-starved relationship, allowing you to maximize the moments you have together and enjoy them more.

Hardcover, Jacketed   0-310-24597-4

Also Available:

0-310-81053-1	Time Together	Hardcover, Jacketed
0-310-26885-0	Your Time-Starved Marriage	Audio CD, Unabridged
0-310-27103-7	Your Time-Starved Marriage Groupware DVD	DVD
0-310-27155-X	Your Time-Starved Marriage Workbook for Men	Softcover
0-310-26729-3	Your Time-Starved Marriage Workbook for Women	Softcover

Love Talk

Speak Each Other's Language Like You Never Have Before

Drs. Les and Leslie Parrott

A breakthrough discovery in communication for transforming love relationships.

Over and over, couples consistently name "improved communication" as the greatest need in their relationships. *Love Talk*—by acclaimed relationship experts Drs. Les and Leslie Parrott—is a deep yet simple plan full of new insights that will revolutionize communication in love relationships.

The first steps to improving this single most important factor in any marriage or love relationship are to identify your fear factors and determine your personal communication styles, and then learn how the two of you can best interact. In this no-nonsense book, "psychobabble" is translated into easy-to-understand language that clearly teaches you what you need to do—and not do—for speaking each other's language like you never have before.

Love Talk includes:

- The Love Talk Indicator, a free personalized online assessment (a $30.00 value) to help you determine your unique talk style
- The Secret to Emotional Connection
- Charts and sample conversations
- The most important conversation you'll ever have
- A short course on Communication 101
- Appendix on Practical Help for the "Silent Partner"

Two softcover "his and hers" workbooks are full of lively exercises and enlightening self-tests that help couples apply what they are learning about communication directly to their relationships.

Hardcover, Jacketed   0-310-24596-6

Also Available:

0-310-80381-0	Just the Two of Us	Hardcover, Jacketed
0-310-26214-3	Love Talk	Audio CD, Abridged
0-310-26467-7	Love Talk Curriculum Kit	DVD
0-310-81047-7	Love Talk Starters	Mass Market
0-310-26212-7	Love Talk Workbook for Men	Softcover
0-310-26213-5	Love Talk Workbook for Women	Softcover

I Love You More

How Everyday Problems Can Strengthen Your Marriage

Drs. Les and Leslie Parrott

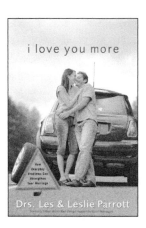

How to make the thorns in your marriage come up roses.

The big and little annoyances in your marriage are actually opportunities to deepen your love for each other. Relationship experts and award-winning authors Les and Leslie Parrott believe that your personal quirks and differences—where you squeeze the toothpaste tube, how you handle money—can actually help draw you together provided you handle them correctly.

Turn your marriage's prickly issues into opportunities to love each other more as you learn how to

- build intimacy while respecting personal space
- tap the power of a positive marriage attitude
- replace boredom with fun, irritability with patience, busyness with time together, debt with a team approach to your finances … and much, much more.

Plus—get an inside look at the very soul of your marriage, and how connecting with God can connect you to each other in ways you never dreamed.

Softcover   0-310-25738-7

Also Available:
0-310-26582-7	I Love You More Curriculum Kit	DVD
0-310-26275-5	I Love You More Workbook for Men	Softcover
0-310-26276-3	I Love You More Workbook for Women	Softcover

Pick up a copy today at your favorite bookstore!

ZONDERVAN®

GRAND RAPIDS, MICHIGAN 49530 USA

WWW.ZONDERVAN.COM

We want to hear from you. Please send your comments about this book to us in care of zreview@zondervan.com. Thank you.

GRAND RAPIDS, MICHIGAN 49530 USA

ZONDERVAN.COM/
AUTHOR**TRACKER**